I0164816

SHADOWS IN THE SUNSET

A Book of Poetry

by Norman Ralph Ross

"These are the gloomy companions of a disturbed imagination; the melancholy madness of poetry..."
Junius

AFTERMATH (A Cinquain)

Alone,

Worried skies frown.

Cataclysmic rain falls,

Slants down across the pane; I weep—

Then drown.

Copyright 2007 Norman Ross.
All rights reserved.

No part of this book may be reproduced,
stored in a retrieval system, or transmitted
by any means without the written permission
of the author.

ISBN: 978-0-6151-7091-6

THE WEDDING

The chill, insistent hands of Death
Reach out and clasp me to her breast;
Her impelling lips are pressed
Against an acquiescent heart.
Close to mine her cheek is resting;
Seductively, her body testing
My waning power to resist
Life's final symphony.

Her perfume vagrantly assails the air,
Its lethal fragrance lures me on
To sooner cross the Rubicon
And lapse into eternal sleep.

Death wants so much to be my wife;
To love her more than I do life;
With words that promise peace,
she seeks to woo
And stem the beating heart.

<u>REFRAIN</u>

Hear the wind? It beckons.
Hark! The night! It calls.
And my heart is dwelling
Where the water falls.
By the sea it wanders,
On the empty shore,
Cloaked in velvet evening
Now and evermore.

Warmed by silken moonbeams,
Yet by shadows fed,
Like the surf it lingers,
Like the surf it's fled.
Always searching, searching,
For a magic place,
Weaving of a snowfall
Necklaces of lace.

Now it seeks the forest,
Now the sheltered glens,
Gently kissing creatures
Curled about their dens.
Up! Into the mountains,
Higher! To a star.
What can be its purpose
Wandering so far?

Always drifting, drifting
Endless as the rain…
I wonder…will it ever
Come back to me again.

<u>VIGNETTE</u>

I saw the sun set, a jelly omelet in a frying pan sky.

I saw a house, too, with brown shingles

Sprawling like tobacco leaves

Over the frame.

It stood alone on a hill. A dark and lonely house.

With stovepipe chimney—A tin soldier

Sitting in a beach chair.

I saw a path that led to the door…

A crooked smile on the dark earth's face.

I saw a face peer through the pane.

Opaque, disfigured, a dumb portrait

On a glass canvass.

I saw dignity. A television antenna

Pedantic, geometric,

Questioning the sky.

Then, pouring over the house

Like coal from a chute

Night came…

I closed my eyes

And saw—nothing.

TO PANDORA

The mountains proud
A puff of cloud
Work's a grind
Love is blind
The smell of pine
A glass of wine
Kissing's sweet
Liquor's neat
A tall white sail
Raising bail
The world's a place
And wins the race
The taste of food
A mellow mood
Dinner at eight
Parades are great
The pangs of love
A furry glove
Take the rod
Thinking's hard
An early Mass
A naked ass
Pick a mate
Though winning's great

A child's delight
The dark of night
And water's cool
But so's a fool
A rose that's red
The warmth of bed
And so is candy
But grass is dandy
The wail of rain
A cry of pain
Where bad gets better
As good gets deader
A dog's wet lick
An "X" skin flick
So get on line
Don't rain on mine
A sunset gold
The champagne's cold
To measure meanness
But not for genius
A bell that's ringing
A choir singing
Of your choosing
I'm mostly losing.

LYRIC AFTER A TEA PARTY

I thought we'd stay together,

And raise a cup of wine,

Perhaps to toast the weather,

And afterwards to dine.

But now I see you're dressing,

Your business must be pressing,

The night you keep on stressing,

Will surely not be mine.

The moon will not get younger,

Its countenance and mine

Are sick and pale with hunger,

For lack of proper chine.

And though we may not show it,

Undoubtedly you know it,

Your presence can bestow it—

A soothing anodyne.

I see you will be hurried,

My pleas you swift decline,

And so you must be worried

About my true design.

I'll tell you of the measure

You are my dearest treasure

It is my earnest pleasure

That love will make you mine.

BEYOND SUNSET

Post-WWII Poetry

*"Masks, hatchets, racks, and vipers…
dance in all the mazes of metaphorical
confusion."*

~Junius

I AM THE LIFE...

They lie who say the stalks of corn are sleeping—
Their midsummer greenness more than
memories
In the wild euphoria of human weeping.

I groped out there in darkness on my knees
Prayerfully clawing kernels in the earth;
In the rites of spring, at least, there is no
dying—
But only sprigs of green and
Tender leaves and
Graceful golden tassels in the sun
of Spring
Exploding toward some unseen star and
Birth.

But silence in a deluge; in a wave!
The corn is ashen, is always dying.
No resurrected Lazarus come from the grave.
But only ritual blood and deathless sighing.

O, will you copulate with Spring?
The corn! Remember?
The corn is dead;

...and the heart is stunned.

RELIVING FLIGHTS

(From Hospital)

I

Recall love, Recall hate,
Recall palm trees, pine trees, oaks.
Recall fate.

Recall dreams,
Recall fears,
Recall oceans, rivers, lakes.
Recall tears.

Dry them, the all consuming oceans,
The rivers,
The lakes.
Dry the seas of tears.
Suck them up through parched lips
Quench the overwhelming thirst -- or die!

II

Recall desire,
Recall lust,
Recall friends, enemies, fleeting acquaintances.
Recall dust.

Recall dark, Recall light,
Recall purple hills, mountains, jagged rocks.
Recall night,
Thunderous rain!
Silent snow!
Deep, misty fog!
Gray, shadowy dusk!
(Recall these)

III

Over bottomless chasms,
Still, soundless villages,
Sleepless cities and sandless deserts,
Over the steaming jungle's sun sprayed beaches.

Over hills, perilous mountains,
Parched fields, fruitless harvests.
Over rotted, rusted ships beneath the
channels
And white-stoned graves and crosses
row on row.

Recall the birth of life!
Recall the advent of Death!
Recall a Mother's womb.
Recall the final breath.

SESTINA FOR WINTER

The city's trees are shriveled, bleak, and bare.
The matted clouds are gray with threatened snow.
The people scurry home in bristling cold
with finger-tips and toes like beaded ice.
One last ribbed leaf goes tumbling in the wind
which fiercely rattles every window glass,

as eager children, huddled to the glass,
peer into the streets now almost bare.
At last, in flurries, it has begun to snow,
and stragglers bundle up against the cold,
(which turns the first few early flakes to ice),
their bodies bent to spear the startling wind.

Frost-fettered branches snapping in the wind
rattle to the street and crack like glass;
And now the frost-packed earth is quick to bare
the swift but silent cataracts of snow
and piercing sleet—and still, so pinching cold,
the river stands amazed and turns to ice.

Thin saplings in the park are cased in ice
and quiver numbly in the aching wind,
much like slim sticks of polished glass
or giant icicles. Stark and lean, they bare
their crystal branches to the glacial snow
and stand imprisoned in the chill, hibernal cold,

naked and lonely. While the parching cold
transforms the wandering rills to paths of ice,
a squirrel trembles in the chattering wind,
treading nimbly on the brooks of glass;
His autumn hollow echoes, being bare
of acorns, or else is blanketed with snow.

How beautifully the earth is banked with snow
and soft white drifts. The world is marble cold
and static—sculptured crystalline in ice—
willing subject for the keen-bladed wind
that burrs and burnishes the lakes, like glass
or iridescent prisms glazed and bare.

Look now! How bare the sky is all of snow,
Though still it's cold; and skaters on the ice
Ignore the wind and skim along the glass.

11

BATTLE FATIGUE

I lay upon a fallow slab, like stone;
My eyes read death within the white-walled room;
The wild mind whirled, in eddies, to despoil
The twisted nerves, the blood, the sallow bone.

They knew no reason for my sense of doom
Those learned doctors of the living soil
The sword, the fire and the blood-red seas
Locked me firmly in a fathomless tomb.

I waited. Cold. Stark as a serpent coil.
No shock. No ice. No words had set me free.
And now, amatol. The watery flume sluiced
Along my veins from a slender foil.

I wept. The blackness funneled through a cone
Of swirling tears. I slept. Alone, alone.

SHADOWS

I walk the streets of foreign soil alone —
And look for you in every street café;
Lovers' laughter bubbles everywhere
Like pink champagne. And flowers, multi-hued,
The golden hyacinth and orange mum,
The purple primrose, like myrrh and frankincense
Pervade the air with fragrance sweet and light—
(Like your body scent one loving carefree night).

And every corner that I turn, I hope
To find you waiting there — in black and white.

I follow endlessly the peopled walks
And turn each way to peer into the crowded shops.
I squint above the sun-sprayed windows
There to find you smiling down on me.
But then you vanish as an image in
A mirrored pool disturbed by pebbles cast.
I wander through the parks along the shore;
I trod the squares and peek through every door

In curiosity. But when night falls, I pause
In silence, to listen to your voice

Once more.

SONNETS FOR THE SUNRISE

A Contemporary Sequence of Elizabethan Sonnets in a New Day

ROSLYN HARBOR I

What hostile wind in spinning vortex blew
Pain into my life? What sullen lark
Gave up its joyful song? What Cain slew
My way in wavering mist and seeling dark?

And all my love, like wine or blood, has drained;
My heart-red hues to ashen white have turned;
The tender seeds so lovingly engrained
Wither in the earth, dust-seared and burned.

Where have they fled, the sparkling springtime
years?
The buds of May and summer's damasked roses?
What wine-ambrosia mingles with my tears
As sun-vined August droops and night encloses?

But now, like starburst in a darkling sky,
My dear love's beauty lightens all that's nigh.

15

ROSLYN HARBOR II

The starlit symphony of cosmic sighs,
or rising suns in dawning-radiant hues
that paint the sky in dappled sea-bright blues
cannot compare in beauty with your eyes,
nor emulate the music of your sighs
when your lips
brush mine.
Divinity imbues
your visage, and
gods extract dear dues
of Love as payment for that Angel guise.

What hope is there for poets such as I
to reach your soul and touch a vibrant string?
Your woman-chord does all too dormant lie,
while my brief wisdom yearns to make you sing.
Yet dead leaves grow; grass turns green; and I
have faith in joys that rolling Time may bring.

ROSLYN HARBOR III

I thank you for these few brief weeks we've had—
But actually, I think they've gone too fast;
I know that when I leave we'll both be sad—
But hopeful that our budding love will last.

I'm not your ordinary kind of man,
But, sui generis to say the least;
In love, I do the very best I can—
I'll rise, like dough, if you supply the yeast!

And if you promise not to make a sound,
I'll marry you (in theory) e'er
we're parted;
Remember, dear, the world's a
circle round—
One usually ends up where one
has started.

So I'll return and marry you, (in fact),
Assuming, of course, our love is still intact.

DARK LOVE

A cold, dark wind has brushed across our path,
and mystic clouds wrack our sun-starved eyes;
A sudden storm in droning thunder's wrath
ricochets and echoes in our skies.

Our love's brief lightning flashes chilling rain
that ripples down the windows
of our hearts.
What cruel whim of nature
drizzles pain
to flood away July before it starts?

But my bleak barometer turns aright,
and weather vanes will spin a better way;
Our sun, though hidden, is somewhere burning
bright;
And love is not a fickle summer's day

for ill winds to shake when e'er they blow;
Our love is young and needs some rain to grow.

GET DRESSED—GO HOME!

Truly, I'm a proper lady living here
on this street for eight relatively quiet years—
(Mostly speaking); raising daughters without fears
until your body forced me to a guilty tear
for caressing you—and messing up my hairdo.
How could I do such a terribly rash thing
as lure your innocence up into my room? There
to—No matter. Certainly not to hear Sinatra sing.

But now I've cooled these wicked, hot
desires;
The answer's not to have you come here
anymore—
(Even though the thought of you ignites
my fires).
The affair is over. C'est finis. So shut the door.
O' God, I don't know what I'm saying. Can this be
true?
Will I be damned in Hell? Is this what Love can
do?

BELL, BOOK AND CANDLE

There is some magic binds me to your eyes--
Witchcraft, born of Sorcery and Guile;
And yet, they look so innocent all the while,
A necromantic, star-bright blue surprise!

Did Merlin out of Camelot devise
the runic incantation of your smile?
Is Circe's song one half so volatile,
enchanting, or bewitching as your sighs?

There's wizardry in sunlight on your hair;
and conjury in the curving of your breast;
You walk and create music everywhere
to cast a spell and leave my heart possessed.

For when you're near, like alchemists of old,
you turn my life's base metal into gold.

FLIGHT

I do not know what others think of love,
But as for me, I have no doubts about it—
Like flowers needing sunlit skies above,
Lacking, both they and I would die without it.

No sun appears now in my starless life;
Black night envelops everything around me.
My home, my children, and a loving wife
I find no longer anywhere around me.

How shall I start anew
in this strange world
Of hostile storms and
blinding winds of
violence?
When shall my banner finally be unfurled?
Whose kiss shall vanquish fear and bitter silence?

Where shall I find the love to overthrow
And banish all my pain? I do not know.

AND SO...FAREWELL

I must leave e'er fragrant gardens fade,
Before the rose's carmine petals blow
At very height of summer's green parade,
And never see the hillsides banked with snow.

I must leave e'er golden corn will rise,
And silver maples still caress their leaves,
Before the gentle sun of autumn dies,
And winter's breath spews ice upon the eaves.

Just so, our love will be at summer's height
When I depart in sadness from your side
For like the summer,
you provide my light,
And sadness is my
winter...light denied.

And for a parting gift to you, my sweet,
I lay this sonnet garland at your feet.

VIKING SONG

When I peer at the sky in Nordic lands,
and tread where pines and fragrant flowers grow;
Or watch the fjords reflect the mountain snow
like silvered glass along the Viking strands;

When I see glaciers trailing to the sun
caressed by dawning's tender summer rays,
and waterfalls in
myriad patterns run
in graceful splendor
down to Nordic bays,

Then I am sad. For all this loveliness
like life, is transient, and is doomed to death
by frozen arctic winds' ice-chilling breath;
So brief is Scandinavia's sun-swept kiss.

Just so, I fear our love, like summer's gold
too soon will turn to frost like winter's cold.

COPENHAGEN I

I am the most unhappy man alive,
wandering across this world alone
to seek a reason why I must survive,
and why my life has turned from blood to stone.

Where is the love to grace my final years?
Where is the love I so dearly crave?
Where is the love to calm my deepest fears?
Who will there be to weep beside my grave?

The beauty that I sought, where did it go?
Shall I be humble and accept the guilt
for fifty years and nothing left to show
but shattered pieces of the life I built?

Of this be certain—I'll pass this searing test;
My heart and soul are clear. I did my best.

BRIGHTON I

Along the English Channel's rock-lined coast
where white-ribbed cliffs stand guard against the
sea;
Where moonlight rifles through a star bright host
to pierce my heart with memories of thee.

I stand where Viking long boats dashed ashore
on Brighton's ancient battle-ridden land,
and listening to the waves' incessant roar,
I reach across the sea to take your hand.

Where Stonehenge Druids sang their mystic rites,
and Romans came t'enslave the Celtic race;
Where Arthur raised up Camelot and knights,
I yearn in silent pain to touch your face.

For I have cast aside all history
to wonder why your love has fled from me.

AMSTERDAM I

On Holland's flowering northern shore, a dike
controls the waters of the Zuider Zee;
But Netherlanders have yet to build the dike
that can contain the love I have for thee.

In Amsterdam, the diamond merchants ply
their ancient art; they polish, cut, and grind
the precious stones, not one of which comes nigh
so precious as the love I left behind.

The locks, the quaint canals, a moonlight cruise,
the windmills slowly winding in the sun;
Where million-tuliped fields, and wooden shoes,
and fragrant roses make your senses run —

These are the things that bring the Dutch such fame
But my love's beauty puts them all to shame.

THE POKER HAND

What can I say before I leave once more?
I wish you knew how much you mean to me —
But unrequited love is such a bore,
one day your eyes will open, and you'll see

My love is numberless, and warm and rich
as Autumn leaves that fall from tired trees.
When you're alone my dear and start to itch,
recall how hard I tried to love you, please.

I thought you needed me; guess I was wrong.
For your cold words keep
ringing in my ear
to chill my lonely flight. So
goes the song.
But spring will come around, and I'll be here

To make my entrance with the usual flair —
One is no number, my love — but two is a pair!

ATHENS I

We were so happy lying side by side —
Now, chill November winds destroy the leaves
as brittle, sere, and dead as one who grieves
for love that briefly flickered and then died.
What boots it now that we both have our pride
and nothing else? Time and Age are thieves
who rob us both of that which one believes;
Love's bliss would be our lot, had we but tried.

How desperately I yearn to see your face,
to touch your hand, to warm your bitter heart;
How cruel you were withholding your embrace
a microsecond ere I would depart.
But I'll have this to comfort me — the grace
and wonder of you while we are apart.

DELPHI I

Why is our love affair so stormy, dear?
I know it's not because I love a fight,
or wish to make Love's conflicts my career —
I also find our quarrels are so trite!

One answer only comes at once to mind —
You must be the one to bear the blame;
My character is known to be the kind
that never causes trouble. I make no claim

therefore to kindling all our battles. Thus,
logic dictates the culprit's surely you.
But my forgiving nature makes no fuss
about your tiny flaws — I love you true.

So, keep on drinking vodka while I drink wine,
and ever on each other's meat we'll dine.

DELPHI II

High in the sacred hills of Peloponnese,
Where Agamemnon ruled a golden race,
In silent majesty, the olive trees
Sparkle in the mist like sea-green lace.

Here, clouds caress the Temples of the gods,
And Delphi to the eternal mountain clings,
While Sparta's army toward Mycenae trods
To plunder Atreus's treasure and Trojan kings.

But all stands mute and silent; the
glory's past,
And only ruin marks the heroic
site;

The hushed observer notes that
naught will last,
And all man's works must turn from day to night.

So while you may, find love to fill your heart —
Too soon, my dear, we too the world depart.

ISTANBUL I

It's but a month, why does it seem a year
since last our eyes met across a table?
In all the world, is mine the only tear
for love that seemed contemporary fable?

I mention this because I wait in vain
for words confirming what we had begun:
"O, darling, when you come home again,
We'll do whatever we have left undone.

"For now you've gone, I recognize my need —
Your love is all that's precious; still flows
In me your body chemistry — your seed;
I hold you deep within me and there love grows."

Not words of yours. I'm such a fool, it seems —
From my lips only come these thoughts.

Just dreams.

JERUSALEM I

When e'er I see Jerusalem's cream-pink stones,
and walk beside Gethsemane's garden rills,
to hear the shofar's holy Sabbath tones
reverberate across Judean hills —

When e'er I muse the Mount of Olives' fate,
where ancient Jewish graves hold Zion's soul
in silent slumber — and centuries await
messiah and the Resurrection's scroll —

When e'er I touch the sacred Western Wall,
and join the sects on Temple Mount in prayer,
Who cry, *"Jerusalem! Jerusalem is all!"*
And feel the strength of Israel in the air —

It's then I yearn for one to share my life —
To take a Hebrew woman for my wife.

JAFFA I

The women that I've loved in all my life —
Why do they torment all my empty dreams?
Is it my destiny to live in strife
And hopeless nights forever, as it seems?

What imperfection hovers over me?
Wherein have I deserved this loveless role?
How am I lacking sensitivity?
What scornful sins lie hidden in my soul?

And of them all, one only now remains
To sanctify the love that fills my heart;
Though she alone can disengage the chains
That bind us to eternities apart,

She chooses, rather, to withhold her breath —
And I? O! I will be consoled by Death.

TEL AVIV I

While Sabbath strollers crowd along the shore,
and lovers fill café's beside the bay,
I cannot hold my tears back anymore,
for I'm alone in Tel Aviv today.

White birds cling to rocks upon the
strand,
Or wing to aerie nests by sea-swept
caves —
Children sculpt their castles in the
sand,
and bathers' laughter rings through salt-capped
waves.

But this Israeli canvas makes me sigh
in silent grief; I stare out to the sea,
and while the sun descends the burning sky,
despair, because you have forsaken me.

Across the world, you sigh and turn in sleeping,
at the instant here that I sprawl weeping.

NEW DELHI I

To be away from home on Christmas Eve
while all the world dissolves in Yuletide mirth —
To wear an empty heart upon my sleeve
in Holy Lands halfway across the earth…

To miss the festive streets, the virgin snow
moonlit on tufted trees; the gay delight
of egg-nog toasts with friends; the mistletoe,
the caroling of children in the night…

To rue not having any gifts to bring —
Not wisdom, gold, nor frankincense or myrrh,
To hear nowhere the Herald Angels sing
of home and joys that come from loving her…

To be devoid of cheer this Christmas season —
Would Christ were here to bear away the reason!

BAGHDAD

The New Year rushes in! Gone is the old —

And tarnished visions of our buried dreams

are resurrected joyfully! It seems

life's dross is magically transformed to gold,

for this New Year will surely break the mold

of bygone years and all the shattered schemes —

The darkling skies are filled with bright new beams

whose hopeful message round the world has rolled

to reach me here on Asia's teeming land.

But soberly, I know the year's new bliss

Can wash away as easily as sand.

So, humbly, all I ask of Fate is this:

To bring me safely home to take your hand,

To touch your face, and then — one tender kiss.

KATMANDU I

A Hindu beggar read my palm today
in Delhi, on my way to Katmandu;
His sandaled feet were caked with mud and clay,
his clothes were rags that wretched bones poked
through.

A voice, high piping, and bright ruby eyes
transfixed me in a formulated gaze—
But comfort came in knowing he was wise,
with visions of my past and future days.

And then he told me that my world was strange,
with powers in life that I had scarcely used;
That soon the patterns of my stars would change,
no longer would my planets be abused.

He paused, and sighed — and I could see he knew
how all my days are filled with love for you.

TAHITI I

I loved you once at summer's verdant height
But left to circumnavigate the globe,
Wondering if the world contained a sight
as tempting as the moment you disrobe.

Topkapi's gems, nor India's Kohinoor,
Nor wandering over Britain's ancient isle,
Nor sailing Persian gulfs to Ban-Shahpur
Can turn me on as does your grace and style.

I gazed in awe at Bali's banyon trees
And Himalayan skies in Katmandu,
I combed for shells in Bora Bora's seas,
And still get off on nothing else but you.

So, if halfway across the earth you beckoned,
I'd speed to you in just a microsecond.

BALI HIGH

When e'er I think of Bali's island skies
melting to the Indonesian Sea,
Or Ketjak monkey dancers' soulful cries,
and Uluwatu sunsets call to me —

When I remember Ramayanan tales,
or Kintimani's lava oozing down,
And visualize the crimson batik sails
in sleepy bays by Denpesari town —

Then I dream of being with you there,
strolling on the beach to comb for shells,
or sipping wine in Sukawati fair
while listening to Besakih Temple bells —

For nowhere here on earth or far above
can ever speak, like Bali speaks, of love.

WAIKIKI I

I've been around the world — so now, it's done;
Whatever I was seeking, I
have found —
The only number's "two".
There is no "one".
And living life alone is quite unsound.

At least my present task is very clear,
And that's to prove that one and one make two—
But it's not easy. Aye, there's the rub, I fear —
To help me with that task I've chosen you.

It may take many months, for you're a cynic
Who feels, apparently, that one is fine;
And so, I'll have to hold a love-in clinic
Until your theory coincides with mine.

At any rate, if two should finally lose,
Perhaps, at least, I'll be the one you
choose.

PHOENIX I

I left Las Vegas shortly after noon,
And reached a stretch of Arizona road
Where silvered cactus caught the desert moon
along a bed where once a river flowed.

I stopped the car and stepped into the night
Where nothing seemed to stir for miles around;
Tumbleweed and cactus, the only sight,
the rush of desert wind, the only sound.

But wondrously, in front of where I stood,
And strange to find such beauty growing here
In barren land, red as Indian blood—
A cactus flower called "Apache Tear".

I thought of you on that moonlit byway--
A desert flower on my lonely highway.

HEMPSTEAD HARBOR

I thought at Hempstead Harbor Beach today
about our summer past, so bittersweet —
How memories of you are incomplete
without the wind and sand, and sun and spray.

I gazed into the blue and wondered there
what joys or tears our futures well might bring,
how warm and bright the beach in early spring,
and how it symbolized our young affair.

I know and love the person that you are:
Mercurial — so like the springtime weather;
Yet, you're my summer sun when we're together,
you are my fixed and constant Morning Star.

And though my spring is gone, and
summer, too,
I'll spend my autumn days in loving
you.

THE PROPOSAL

I know you look ahead with trepidation,
And fear, perhaps, you'll make a wrongful choice;
There is no need for so much consternation,
If only you would heed your inner voice.

For if its love you really want and need,
Open up your heart while life is blessing you;
Why follow endlessly your lonely creed
When there's a man you know who loves caressing
you?

Our lives bring disappointments
hard enough
Without creating artificial strife;
And though, no doubt, you'll
hang in very tough,
Resign yourself—one day you'll
be his wife.

And even though you might not care for it,
I think, at least, you should prepare for it.

43

EPILOGUE

TELL ME, WHICH IS THE WAY TO ITHACA?

Love:
My love is as the love of Heroes
For I have conquered the World
And moved the Stone of Sisyphus
And my house is the house of the High Tower
    I am not an anachronism
    On the running heel of Time:
    For Today and Tomorrow
    I am the wind of Camelot
    The rain of Troy
Flooding you with a hero's love.

Are you not Isolde of the White Flower
Whom I, as Poet, reach out to touch with my wild
kiss?

Do you rather turn majestically away
    From dreams
And burn the Poems behind you?
The sun you love is at your back
Behind the window of your house
The shadows fall across the soil-white pages
    Of non-words
And there, chained upon the Hearth
You busy yourself
Waiting, waiting…
A Penelope out of Time, living

Not Poetry, but
The news of the day.

Ah! My love!
On the beach
Where the never ending surge of water
Changes
The face of earth again and again
Each minute of the day, night, and always
Then and there when I recall the change in this
thing called
Me…
The new sides, new forms, new shapes of me
Which came when you washed across my being
Like a wave retreating to the wine-dark sea
I will think of you.

For you disappear in the mist
Around a far corner
In a green Impala
And you are not of my house
The house of the High Tower
And I who have been touched by the eternal
spark—
A Tristram, a Leander, and Odysseus
For me there is nothing left to do
But return to my house
There to lie in the street
And toss grapes at the moon.

...and so to bed.
Alexander Pope

Find Your Favorite Poem

Poetry Format Created by: Barbara and Joel M. Ross

www.ingramcontent.com/pod-product-compliance
Lightning Source LLC
Chambersburg PA
CBHW030304030426
42337CB00012B/586